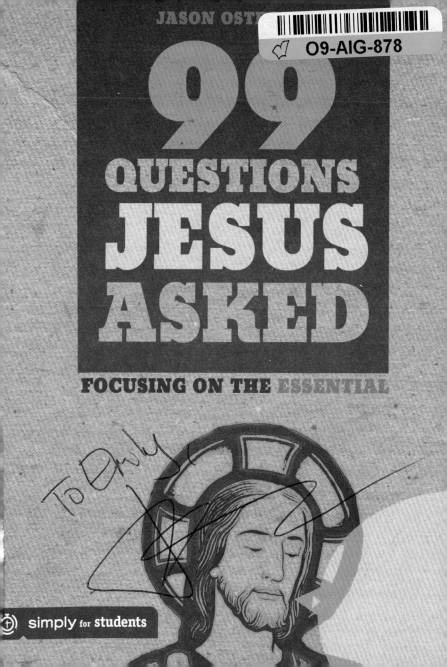

99 Questions Jesus Asked
Focusing on the Essential

© 2012 Jason Ostrander

group.com
simplyyouthministry.com

Credits
Author: Jason Ostrander
Executive Developer: Nadim Najm
Chief Creative Officer: Joani Schultz
Copy Editor: Rob Cunningham
Cover Art and Production: Veronica Preston

ISBN 978-0-7644-8252-6

10 9 8 7 6 5   20 19 18 17 16 15 14 13

Printed in the United States of America.

To Calu, Liam, and Jams...

CONTENTS

Introduction i

Questions 1-10 1

Questions 11-20 11

Questions 21-30 21

Questions 31-40 31

Questions 41-50 41

Questions 51-60 51

Questions 61-70 61

Questions 71-80 71

Questions 81-90 81

Questions 91-99 91

INTRODUCTION

If you are ever in a conversation with someone and want to appear smarter, there is one surefire way to make it happen: Answer that person's question with a question. Seriously, try it! The next time a friend asks, "How are you doing today?" look back with a tilted head and one eye opened wider than the other and ask, "How are *you* doing today?" Automatically you will seem like the one with all the knowledge because you know something that your friend doesn't. Hilarious! But all kidding aside, asking questions is one of the oldest forms of teaching, and Jesus was the master of asking the right questions.

In this book we are going to explore 99 different questions that Jesus asked. That may seem like a lot of questions, but the Gospels record more than 300 questions from him! By just looking into the questions that Jesus asked, we will be able to focus on the things that were super important to Jesus. After each question, you'll find a very quick explanation as to the context of the question, which will be followed by an immediate response. The best way to use these questions is to keep them on your mind throughout the day—meditate on them and, ultimately, answer them.

The majority of the questions that Jesus asked were not meant to be rhetorical (not needing an answer); they were meant to be answered in real time, by real people. The same holds true today. Jesus' words in the Gospels are to be taken seriously by all those who read them. One last thing: All of the questions have the corresponding verse with them; I encourage you to have a Bible handy to read the paragraph before and after the question so you can get the bigger picture of what's going on in the stories. OK, so the real question now is, what will you do with all these questions?

Before we begin, let's first talk about why it's so important that the writers of the Gospels included so many of Jesus' questions.

There are three things that make Jesus' teaching style of "question asking" so powerful. First, if you ask a question, you're displaying a genuine interest in the person. Everything that Jesus said was perfect and timely (because he was the Son of God), and he wasn't asking questions to get answers necessarily—rather, he was relating to the people on a very deep level. Just because he might have known the answer already doesn't mean he was being disingenuous; instead, he was using questions to illuminate what he knew were the real issues in people's lives.

Second, by leaving a legacy of questions rather than a list of answers (or to-do's), Jesus was communicating how important it was to think as a Christian. For Jesus it was more important that he teach us *how* to think than to tell us *what* to think!

Finally, the fact that Jesus asked so many questions helps us know that we have a role in this whole Christian life. Most world religions have, at their core, leaders who make statement after statement about how their followers should live their lives, which would require an almost robot-like response disconnected from the leader. But Jesus' approach with his followers was to put them in the game by seeking their responses and working with their answers right on the spot!

Now on to the questions...

QUESTION #1

"If you love those who love you, what reward will you get?" – Matthew 5:46

This question is as important today as it was 2,000 years ago. In Matthew 5, Jesus was trying to help the disciples think differently about who they should love. Any one of us can love those who love us, but what do we do with the people who ignore us? As Christians, if we're looking for a pat on the back because we love those closest to us, we're not going to get it. That's called being rewarded for following the status quo (in other words, everyone already does it). Instead we should be seeking those outside of our friend circle to pray for.

Draw a circle on a piece of paper and write the names of your closest friends. Now draw a bigger circle surrounding the first circle. Ask God to bring people's names to mind that you would rarely encounter on a given day but that you feel like you should be praying for. Write their names within the larger circle, and commit to regularly praying for them.

"Who of you by worrying can add a single hour to his life?" – Matthew 6:27

Worry can be defined as being tormented with cares or anxiety. To worry about something is not always a good thing—unless the object of your "worrying" or fixation is the kingdom of God. One of Jesus' primary objectives here on earth was to constantly direct our eyes away from those things we have no control over (the created) to the one who has all of the control (the Creator).

Stare at a clock, preferably one without a second hand, for one full minute. Once the minute has passed, ask yourself, "What did I do to cause that to happen?" At its core, that is a very profound (and deep) question, but one that Jesus says is a waste of time. What if we were to take our ability to worry about ourselves and start focusing on the things of God? In other words, what if we started casting all of our cares and anxieties upon him?

QUESTION #3

"And why do you worry about clothes?"
– Matthew 6:28

Have you ever wondered why there isn't a lot written about
what Jesus looked like or what kind of clothes he wore? (It
is interesting, given that he is one of the most talked about
people in history!) Perhaps it was because Jesus understood
the difficulty of being led by what other people thought was
attractive. In Matthew 6 Jesus was attempting to redirect
the attention of his followers back to God's ability to
provide for them.

Jesus Christ was neither anti-clothes (obviously, because
he wore them), nor anti-fashion (whatever the majority
of people were wearing in that day, so was he). His main
concern was the amount of time people spent worrying
about these things. Take a minute and look at yourself in
the mirror, and ask God what would be attractive to
him today.

QUESTION #4

"Do people pick grapes from thornbushes, or figs from thistles?" – Matthew 7:16

Often Jesus would use things that were most common in his day to make a point. Grapes can be easily picked off of luscious rows in a vineyard, or you can go hunting for them in thornbushes. The grapes would taste the same; it's just that one would be easier to get than the others. When Jesus asked this question, he wasn't trying to teach the fine art of grape harvesting; rather, he was relating the different ways that we look for truth.

As a Christian it is easy to look for truth in many places. No doubt, we can see the handiwork of God when we look at the mountains during a sunset, or stare out over a vast ocean, or even when we have spiritual conversations with our friends—but that cannot be the only place we search for truth. The easiest (and most accessible) place to find it is in God's Word. In what ways are you using the Bible as our truth source, or are you constantly looking for truth in more difficult situations?

QUESTION #5

"Why do you look at the speck of sawdust in your brother's eye and pay no attention to the plank in your own eye?" – Matthew 7:3

We've all done it—the classic "XYZ." We wince at the thought of someone telling us that our zipper's down. Imagine, though, if you were caught with your zipper down right after critiquing what someone else was wearing! No matter how fashionably you were dressed, it would only take one zipper down to undo the whole thing.

This picture is similar to the one that Jesus was trying to make when he talked about a plank in the eye. Jesus' question reminds us that we should be very careful not to criticize others while we have such obvious faults of our own. It's not that we can't give advice or critique, but trying to do so without addressing our own issues doesn't make any sense! Here is a good question to ask yourself today: "If all Christians in this world acted like me, would that be good or bad for Christianity?"

QUESTION #6

"Why are you so afraid?" – Matthew 8:26

Did you know that there are more than 500 official phobias referenced by medical professionals? Did you know that agyrophobia is the fear of crossing the street? Or that cathisophobia is the fear of sitting? Fear is an interesting thing—it can instill panic, hysteria, or even greater irrationalities, but it can also bring us to dependency on something that is greater than what we fear.

You cannot avoid all of the storms in your life. The disciples found this out the hard way when they got caught up in an actual storm with Jesus while on a boat. The answer to his question of why they were so afraid was obvious to all the other people in the boat. But it only took one simple command from Jesus to calm the storm—and likewise, it will only take one simple command from him to calm the storm you're experiencing today or will experience down the road. How have the storms of life driven you closer to or further away from the one who is stronger than anything you fear?

QUESTION #7

"Why do you entertain evil thoughts in your hearts?" – Matthew 9:4

Think about things that entertain you: video games, television, cell phones, books, sports, music. The point of entertainment is to capture your full attention. The more you pay attention to something, the more you'll pay! (BTW, this is a great marketing principle!) Did you know that your heart has an eye for entertainment and wants to be fully engaged in something?

A heart-level engagement is the prized possession for any object. In this scene, Jesus was questioning the Pharisees on the condition of their heart. He wanted to know exactly why they chose to allow their hearts to be entertained by evil rather than good. What amazing things did the Pharisees miss because of their wrong hearts? What might you be entertaining in your heart that could keep you from seeing Christ at work today?

QUESTION #8

"How can the guests of the bridegroom mourn while he is with them?" – Matthew 9:15

It's hard to ignore the party that happens in Times Square in New York City every New Year's Eve. All of the fanfare, the celebrities, the bands—it may be the greatest party in the world. Think about the last party that you attended or threw—what things made it "hard to ignore"? Was it the music, the people, the food, or the setting? Whenever people organize parties—especially weddings—they want them to be remarkable.

As Jesus was talking to the disciples in this passage, he asked a question about a bridegroom at a wedding. Of course he wasn't talking about an actual wedding, but he was referring to the crazy notion of mourning the loss of the groom before he leaves the party! Just like the bridegroom should be hard to ignore at a wedding, Jesus should be hard to ignore in our lives. Does this describe our relationship with Jesus—that in spite of everything going on in our lives, Jesus is hard to ignore?

QUESTION #9

"Do you believe that I am able to do this?"
– Matthew 9:28

Take all the cash that you have right now and put it on the table in front of you. Count it up and then think about this for a moment: "What will I do with this money?" Perhaps it will pay for lunch or coffee or even a new video game. Regardless of what your money will buy, it is useless for its intended purpose until it is invested in it. For example, I could eat a dollar bill, but it would taste a lot better if I invested it in a value menu item at McDonald's®!

Jesus' question about whether or not we believe that he can do the miraculous could also be understood like this: Are you willing to invest your faith in me? What are you investing you faith in? Our faith in and of itself can't accomplish anything; rather it is the one we invest it in that makes it so powerful. Oftentimes we are quick to invest faith in ourselves or in our friends, but what about investing it in Jesus? Are you willing to say that he is able to do it?

QUESTION #10

"What did you go out [into the desert] to see?"
– Matthew 11:8

Look back at your three most recent Facebook® status updates. What were you wanting people to see about you? Did it have something to do with what you were wearing or something to do about how you were feeling?

This question Jesus asked in Matthew was in reference to the way people perceived his friend John the Baptist. People had heard about John but hadn't met him, so when they did finally meet him, they were shocked to see that he was not the person they assumed he would be. Likewise, people assumed that Jesus was someone that he was not (such as a general, a warrior, or a politician). Jesus always busted through the expectations that people had of him— much like John the Baptist did. In a world that expects you to focus on yourself, what are you doing to break those expectations? More specifically, how can you use your status updates on Facebook to break the culture's expectations?

QUESTION #11

"To what can I compare this generation?"
– Matthew 11:16

If your house is like mine, you probably have a wall with
a bunch of framed pictures of family members. Wherever
those pictures may be located, take a good look at them for
a minute. Some of the people you may know, others you
may not. Some of the people in the pictures may seem so
foreign to you because the picture was taken so long ago—
especially if the picture is in black and white! Those older,
unrecognizable pictures were taken of people in a
different generation.

When we read through the Gospels, we find that Jesus
was very concerned with individual people—that's one
reason why so many individual healings were recorded.
Often Jesus would talk about large groups of people or even
generations of people. With this particular question, Jesus
was expressing frustration with his generation for its lack of
spiritual maturity. Have you ever thought about what your
generation will be known for in the future? Thinking in a
generational way should be both an encouragement and
a challenge. Be encouraged that you are not alone, but be
challenged to do great things as a generation in Jesus' name.
To what will *your* generation be compared?

"If any of you has a sheep and it falls into a pit on the Sabbath, will you not take hold of it and lift it out?" – Matthew 12:11

The invention of social networking truly has made a deep impact on our world. Probably the most amazing thing about it is the ability to know how all of our friends are feeling at the same time. If people are being real and honest online, then we have a unique opportunity to minister in a way that Christians in previous generations could not. Pick 10 of your closest friends and look at their five most recent Facebook status updates. What do their updates say about them? How would you say they are doing based on their most recent entry?

On the Sabbath during Jesus' time, it was forbidden to do things like heal people, collect food, or even save a sheep that had fallen into a pit—yet Jesus encouraged all of these things by his own actions. In so many ways, Jesus was trying to encourage his followers to think differently about what was conventional. Just like it was unconventional for Jesus to ask a question like this, what are the unconventional places for you to show love and mercy? The conventional places may be at church youth group or the cafeteria at school—but what about showing love and mercy in new ways? Take those 10 friends that you researched on Facebook a moment ago; how could you show love and mercy to them online?

QUESTION #13

"How can you who are evil say anything good?"
– Matthew 12:34

One of the greatest (and simplest) pranks I've ever seen is when someone replaces the soda in someone's can with water when they're not looking. It is amazing how quickly someone will spit something out of their mouth even though they have tasted water thousands of times before. The simple principle behind this prank is that no matter what the label says, it's what's inside that counts!

Likewise, if you want to know what somebody loves, just listen to that person talk. Here in Matthew 12, Jesus said that out of the overflow of our hearts, our mouths speak. The reason for this is that the things that we store up in our hearts—people, activities, objects, desires—are generally the things we end up talking about. We have to be very careful about the things we let affect us at the heart level, because ultimately these will be the things we are known for. This is the reason Jesus asked this question. People who store up evil things in their heart have a very difficult time saying anything good. What if someone followed you around all day with a microphone? What would that recording say about what you have in your heart?

"Who is my mother, and who are my brothers?"
– Matthew 12:48

Have you ever heard of the "Uncle Syndrome"? Allow me to explain: When I was younger my parents would introduce one of their friends as "uncle" Jim or "aunt" Susan. The interesting thing about this was that the person was not really related to me like my other "real" aunts and uncles. By applying the "Uncle Syndrome" to different individuals, my parents were demonstrating just how important they were—as important as a real aunt or uncle.

Jesus was fully aware who his "real" mother and brother were; it's not like he forgot, but when asked about his mother, Jesus responded with this really weird question. But when we consider the "Uncle Syndrome," we quickly realize that Jesus was communicating that people who follow the will of God are as important as his "real" mother and brother. Assuming that you treat your family properly, are you treating your fellow Christians as mothers and fathers, sisters and brothers?

QUESTION #15

"Have you understood all these things?" – Matthew 13:51

Take a minute to be quiet and listen to all the background noise in your life right now. After 60 seconds, grab a piece of paper and list out *what* noises you can hear. After you've listed them all, try to identify *where* each is coming from. Finally, select one of the noises and try to explain *how* the noise is being made. This simple exercise will help to move you from hearing to listening and then from listening to understanding.

When Jesus traveled around and talked with his disciples, he wanted them to not just hear what he was saying, but also to understand it. This is why Jesus asked this question in Matthew 13. As Christians, we ought to be people who read the Bible. As a student, whenever I would read the Bible, it very rarely went beyond reading to understanding. If Jesus were to confront us today about our time spent reading the Bible, he would surely ask, "Have you understood all these things?" not "Have you read all these things?" Echoing the exercise you did a moment ago, what could you do today to move from reading the Bible to understanding the Bible?

QUESTION #16

"You of little faith, why did you doubt?"
– Matthew 14:31

By now someone has come up to you and asked, "Have you seen that video online where the kid [fill in the blank with the most amazing viral video ever made]?" To which you've said, "No way, that never happened!" Then your friend says, "No really; here—watch," and after you saw the video, you became a believer. The interesting thing about this scenario (which happens every day all over the world) is the thing that led you to belief was your initial doubt. Doubt can be a very powerful thing. It can be the one thing that keeps you from doing things in this life. Yet doubt can also be one of the greatest motivators for trust.

Peter was courageous enough to trust in Jesus' ridiculous request to walk on water regardless of how much doubt surrounded the situation. After the first couple of steps outside the boat, Peter started to focus on the wind and the waves, and doubt caused him to sink into the water below him. After Jesus reached down and lifted Peter out of the water and placed him back into the boat, the most amazing thing happened: The disciples proclaimed that Jesus truly was the Son of God. Peter's doubt motivated the disciples to the fullest form of trust. What doubts do you currently have that could become a motivator to trusting in Jesus through faith?

QUESTION #17

"Why do you break the command of God for the sake of your tradition?" – Matthew 15:3

You probably aren't old enough to have created deeply rooted traditions for your life, but there are some things you do every day just out of tradition. Consider your morning rituals, for example. Take a minute and list all the things that you do every morning before you head out the door (check phone, take a shower, get dressed, brush your teeth, drink coffee, and so on). The truth is that we are people of tradition, and those traditions not only dictate our daily lives, but over time they can become the things that define us.

This is why Jesus asked the Pharisees such a harsh question. As a group the Pharisees were known by their lifestyle of strictly following religious traditions. Their traditions became so important to them that they would give more attention to those traditions than they would give to the God that the traditions supposedly honored! It is very tragic yet very easy to do. What traditions have formed or are beginning to form in your life that may one day keep you from the commands of God? What can you do now to make sure that doesn't happen?

QUESTION #18

"How many loaves do you have?"
– Matthew 15:34

The setting for this question was probably one of the most well-known in the entire Bible. It occurred when Jesus fed thousands of people with only seven loaves of bread and a few small fish. I am willing to bet that they were a bit confused by how Jesus handled this situation. Why did Jesus need to use the small amount of bread and fish anyway? Was there something in those loaves? Couldn't Jesus just snap his fingers and pull the food out of thin air?

The simple observation here is that Jesus used the small amount that the people had and did something greater. Sometimes we get confused into thinking that our small— or seemingly small—talents and gifts won't amount to anything for God. Look around your room; what do you see that could symbolize the talents and gifts you can offer to Jesus? What talents and gifts do you have that Jesus could multiply? In other words, how many loaves do you have?

QUESTION #19

"Who do people say the Son of Man is?" – Matthew 16:13

Did you know that well over 1,000 movies have been produced about Jesus and tens of thousands of books have been written about him? There are a lot of people out there who have an opinion of who Jesus really is. That's what makes this question so important. Jesus didn't ask this question of the disciples so that he could prove or disprove their answer; rather he was interested in their perspective.

As Christians we often think that our responsibility is to tell people who Jesus is, but we also have an opportunity to listen to what other people say about him. Jesus knew that he wouldn't be the only one speaking for himself, but that others would also speak about him. Have you ever taken the time to ask your friends who they think Jesus is? You might be surprised by how little (or how much) your friends know about him. Either way this is a wonderful way to begin a conversation about Jesus with people you meet every day.

QUESTION #20

"But what about you? Who do you say that I am?" – Matthew 16:15

For this question, we will need to go back to elementary school. Do you remember the first time you saw one of your teachers outside of school? Do you remember where it happened: at the grocery store, a restaurant, or maybe the movie theater? If you're like me, you were struck by the realization that your teacher actually had a real life outside of the classroom! (As a kid I thought teachers just lived at school!) This realization is similar to what the disciples were wrestling with when Jesus asked them: Who do you say that I am?

He had just finished asking them who other people thought the Son of Man was (see Question #19), but now he was asking them something personal. By asking this direct question, Jesus was helping the disciples understand something fundamental: that Jesus was not just the Son of God in a grand, "out-there" sort of way, but he also was the personal God who was "down here." As children, when we see teachers out in the real world, we are brought into the bigger picture of their lives. Likewise Jesus is constantly bringing us into the bigger picture of his life. How can you make this "down here" Jesus more of a reality today?

QUESTION #21

"What good will it be for a man if he gains the whole world but forfeits his soul? Or what can a man give in exchange for his soul?"
– Matthew 16:26

Stuff. We all have it, we all buy it, and we all need it. (Well, at least we think we do!) Whether it is a physical collection of stuff like Star Wars® figures, baseball cards, or clothes, or an emotional collection of stuff like memories, hurtful interactions, or experiences, it can be very easy to fall into the trap of collecting "stuff." Many of us struggle to balance the stuff in our lives along with the stuff of our souls. The more stuff we collect in this world, the more we're often left with feelings of emptiness and dissatisfaction.

The question that Jesus asked here gets right to the heart of our desire to collect (or gain) things of this world. How sad it would be to get to the end of our lives and all we have to show for our time on earth is a pile of temporary, disposable things. Think about the last five things you've purchased. Ask yourself this question: "How do these purchases affect my soul?" In other words, how does this make you feel? Are you better for having it? Jesus really isn't beating around the bush here.

QUESTION #22

"O unbelieving and perverse generation, how long shall I stay with you?" – Matthew 17:17

Does it ever seem like there were a lot more miracles being performed during Jesus' time on earth than we see today? So many passages in the Gospels contain some kind of miraculous healing or feeding that it leaves us asking, "Where are those great miracles now?" Is it possible that more people would believe in Jesus if they could see similar miracles today?

When Jesus asked this question, it was more in the rhetorical sense. In other words, it was a question that no one was supposed to answer out loud. Jesus was a healer and could do miraculous things, but nothing was more miraculous than taking away the sins of humanity. Jesus knew that he came to earth to do so much more than just heal paralyzed people or restore sight to the blind, but it was hard for people to see beyond this. It was hard for people to see Jesus as Savior—and this must have been frustrating to Jesus. In what ways have you been guilty of wanting miracles more than wanting the miracle maker?

QUESTION #23

"Why do you ask me about what is good?"
– Matthew 19:17

Take a second and think about all the things that you do differently because you are a Christian. How is your life different because you are involved in youth group? What are the different good things that you do because you are committed to living out this Christian life? On a piece of paper, list as many of those things as you can.

In this Matthew 19 passage, Jesus was talking to a rich, young ruler. This young man was someone who had invested all of his life in being a good person. When he asked Jesus if there was anything he had forgotten to do (so that he could be sure he was going to heaven) Jesus responded with a question of his own. Jesus was trying to focus this good person on the one who is good (Jesus) rather than the good things he could do. How might you fall into the same trap as the young ruler? How can you better focus your life on Christ as opposed to just doing good things for him?

QUESTION #24

"Can you drink the cup I am going to drink?"
– Matthew 20:22

Christ's suffering is pretty much a foreign concept to most of us. As a teenager it is possible that you might endure some form of suffering, but often it relates to the consequences of choices you've made or something that is going on with friends or family. It would be impossible, though, for any of us to fully understand taking on suffering for all of humanity. It would be just as difficult to relate to the suffering that Christ endured as he bore the weight of our sins on that cross.

At times we lose sight of Jesus as the "great suffering one" who took the cup that God gave him to drink. Only Christ could drink that cup, the contents of which directly relate his death, burial, and resurrection. No one else could handle it. Let us remember the sufferings of Christ today.

QUESTION #25

"What do you want me to do for you?"
– Matthew 20:32

Have you ever received a gift and after opening it, you
thought to yourself, "Why on earth did they get me *this*?"
It's amazing how some people can be so excited about
giving gifts that they don't even really care whether or not
the person they bought it for really likes (or needs) it. This is
probably why the gift receipt was invented!

The interaction between Jesus and the two blind men in
Matthew 20 is so beautiful because it shows us Jesus as a
thoughtful healer. It seems quite obvious what two blind
men would want the healer to do for them, but Jesus still
took the time to consider their desires. As we attempt to
live like Christ—a life of good deeds and grace—let us
always consider the person before we consider the good
deed we want to do. What real need can you meet for
someone today? How will you find out what that need is?

QUESTION #26

"Have you never read in the Scriptures...?"
— Matthew 21:42

When was the last time you tried to put something together without first reading the directions? Maybe it was a bookshelf, or a new bike. We all have confidence at the beginning of a project that we can figure out things like this on our own, only to discover halfway through that we need to consult the directions to complete the task. This same trap can apply to our Christian lives when it comes to our understanding of the Bible.

When Jesus asked this question of his followers, he was emphasizing the importance of actually reading Scripture. It is discouraging to think that so many people in churches today—including teenagers—are attempting to live out their Christian faith without a desire to read God's Word. This may sound a little harsh, but there is no Christian life apart from the Word of God. Don't concern yourself with how much you read the Bible; rather, let your life be marked by how often the Bible changes you when you read it.

QUESTION #27

"You hypocrites, why are you trying to trap me?"
– Matthew 22:18

Have you ever had to set a mousetrap before? You know, the kind with the spring-loaded bar and the little metal tray that you load up with cheese? Setting one of these traps can be a very interesting undertaking—mostly because we're always worried that we'll get our own fingers caught! It is also interesting because the mouse we're trying to catch is only concerned with the bait (cheese) but could care less about the person setting the trap.

Mice would be a lot harder to trap if they were more concerned about the intent of the one setting the trap as opposed to getting the delicious cheese used as bait. When Jesus asked the guards in Matthew 22 why they were trying to trap him, he was not concerned about the trap they were trying to set; rather Jesus was concerned about the one who was setting the trap. (Which is why he would never truly be caught!) Have you ever said things like, "Jesus, if you do this, then I will…"? If so, what are you setting Jesus up for? How would you approach Jesus differently if you knew he was more concerned about you than about if/then type questions?

QUESTION #28

"How will you escape being condemned to hell?"
– Matthew 23:33

Some questions that Jesus asked need very little explanation.
This would be one of them. Jesus asked this question in full
hearing of the Pharisees (the ultra-religious people of his
day). Interestingly enough, whenever he did ask questions
like this one, it was rarely asked of nonreligious people.

By asking this question, Jesus made a direct connection
between people who think they can get out of hell on their
own and people who have lived a religious lifestyle. In
today's terms, Jesus asks those of us who go to church a lot
how we plan on escaping judgment at the end of our lives
here on earth. In other words, does all of our involvement
at church draw us away from relying on Jesus to be the
one who helps us escape hell? The simple answer to this
question is that without Jesus, it is impossible to escape hell.
Jesus didn't mess around with this question—and neither
should we.

"Why are you bothering this woman?"
– Matthew 26:10

What do you know about tithing? How do you determine how much money to put into the offering plate at church, or how much time to give for serving in your church? When Jesus asked his disciples this question in Matthew 26, at first it seems like a respect issue, but as we look deeper, we discover that it is an offering issue. The woman from this passage was offering something very expensive to Jesus, and those watching felt like it was too great of an offering, too much of a sacrifice.

This question from Jesus reminds us that there is nothing that is too good (no amount to high) that we could offer to him. Sometimes we think that anything we can offer to Christ has to fit into those offering plates (or bags or buckets) that get passed around on Sunday morning. Is it possible that we are caught in the mentality of giving Christ a percentage of our time and money—and once we hit that amount, we believe we have nothing more to do? What more could you do that might cause others around you to say, "Don't do that; it's way too much"?

QUESTION #30

"Could you men not keep watch with me for one hour?" – Matthew 26:40

Have you ever heard one of those emergency broadcasts over the TV or radio? Have you ever been in a public building when the fire alarm went off? When things like that occur, it's funny how our first reaction is often to do nothing at all—even in the face of possible danger! Sometimes in life we lack a sense of urgency that would ultimately make us react to potentially harmful situations.

When Jesus came back from praying and found that the disciples who were supposed to be watching out for him were asleep on the ground, he asked this very pointed question. He was frustrated that they lacked a sense of urgency—especially since it was so close to his crucifixion! As Christians we must carry a certain sense of urgency with us (the Bible refers to it as *expectancy*) during our time on this earth. How can you add a sense of urgency to your relationship with God today? In turn, what would God have you feel urgent about today?

QUESTION #31

"Do you not think I cannot call on my Father, and he will at once put at my disposal more than twelve legions of angels?" – Matthew 26:53

I can remember many times when I beat my dad at arm-wrestling competitions as a kid. I can also remember the day that I realized he had been letting me win all along—which then made me rethink all of those one-on-one basketball games I won by just a point (maybe I wasn't ready for the NBA draft at age 10). On some level, when Christ allowed himself to be taken captive in this garden scene, it must have had a similar effect on everyone around.

Jesus could have overcome his arrest in the garden (he could've called on 12,000 angels for help!) but he was submitting to a higher calling from his Father. Jesus showed us that submission is not a form of weakness; rather, it is a form of devotion to a higher calling. How are you submitting your strength and your will to God's higher call on your life today?

"My God, my God, why have you forsaken me?"
– Matthew 27:46

This may be one of the most recognizable questions ever asked by Jesus—mostly because it was stated by Jesus while he was hanging on the cross. It was a passion-filled question intended to communicate both the darkness of the moment as well as the promise of Scripture. No doubt Christ felt abandoned in that moment of agony, but as he quoted from the psalms, it assured him of the great importance of the situation.

The most amazing thing about this question is the way Jesus paired the pain and darkness of a difficult situation with the promise of Scripture. It can be so easy for us to concentrate on only the pain and agony in our lives and completely ignore the help God has given to us. What difficult situation do you need to pair with the promise of God's Word today? How would your life look different if you always looked to Scripture as your help in a time of need?

QUESTION #33

"Why are you thinking these things?" – Mark 2:8

Have you ever been to a magic show or seen a great magician on TV? I absolutely love watching a magic trick being performed, but I am also so skeptical about how it all works! The entire time the magician is performing, I am constantly trying to look for the string, or the mirrors helping to create the illusion. Why do I do that? Why can't I just enjoy the trick for what it is? Sometimes we take this very same skepticism into our relationship with Jesus.

Here in Mark 2, a paralyzed man was lowered through the roof of a house where Jesus was inside preaching. Interestingly enough, it was the paralyzed man's sins that Jesus healed first, not his physical body—which made doubters of the people who witnessed it. Their skeptical thinking got in the way of seeing how beautiful it was that Jesus healed a man's sins. When has your skeptical thinking about Jesus blinded your ability to see his great works? What can you do to change that today?

QUESTION #34

"Which is easier: to say to the paralytic, 'Your sins are forgiven,' or to say, 'Get up, take your mat and walk'?" – Mark 2:9

There are certainly times, both now and 2,000 years ago, when people wondered, "Who is Jesus really?" People have questioned whether or not Jesus was the compassionate healer who gave sight to the blind or the one sent to take away sins. For a long time, many people have said that he is either one or the other. Not so for your generation. Your generation is comfortable with him being *both* a compassionate healer *and* the Savior of the world.

When Jesus asked this rhetorical "which is easier" question, he was proclaiming his ability to be both healer and Savior at one time. Likewise we should live out a "both/and" style of Christianity. Not only should we seek opportunities in this world to help those who cannot help themselves, but we also must be ready to communicate the power of the gospel at any moment. Is God asking you to develop a "both/and" relationship with someone today?

"Do you bring in a lamp to put it under a bowl or a bed?" – Mark 4:21

Think about something that you practice a lot. Maybe it's a sport, or a musical instrument—whatever it is, ask yourself why you practice it. Is it to get better at it, or to be a better performer? More than likely, whatever you're practicing for will be on display one day. Now imagine practicing something your whole life and never revealing it to anybody. Sounds weird, right?

This is the very point that Jesus was trying to make by asking this question. There is an aspect of our Christian life that must be on display. Sure, we are encouraged to approach God on a one-on-one level, but we are also encouraged to demonstrate our Christlikeness with the world around us. The good news of Christ in us should never be a secret. How can you put this into practice today?

QUESTION #36

"Who touched my clothes?" – Mark 5:30

We all know that person at the party—the one who is talking five times louder than anyone else. Or the person at the library that is completely unable to whisper and keeps getting "the look" from the librarian. Sometimes these people are just trying to draw attention to themselves, but other times it is because they aren't very self-aware (in other words, they don't actually realize that they are being so loud). Having good self-awareness is key to growing in maturity in the Christian life.

Jesus knew who he was. No matter the situation, Jesus was aware of his audience, his surroundings, and, most importantly, himself. This question in Mark 5 is a great example of Jesus' self-awareness. Even though a crowd of people surrounded him, Jesus was keenly aware that someone touched him in order to receive power. Have you ever connected self-awareness with your Christian life? How would your daily life change if you became more attuned to your surroundings?

QUESTION #37

"Why all this commotion and wailing?"
– Mark 5:39

When was the last time you got really emotional about something? Maybe it was the loss of a family member, or a broken relationship, but whatever the case, it is easy to lose perspective in the midst of these moments. When Jesus asked this question in Mark 5 it was during an emotional moment for a man named Jarius. Jarius' daughter had just died, and he was asking Christ to heal her. When Jesus arrived on the scene, it was chaotic; everyone was focused on the dead girl rather than the healer who had just entered the room.

Interestingly enough, when Jesus proclaimed that she was not dead, but merely asleep, the crowd laughed at him. They laughed at the Son of God. When we only focus on the commotion around us, there is the chance that we'll miss the fact that Jesus is there. Is there a situation in your life that has blinded you from the presence of Jesus? Do you need a change in perspective to take your attention away from all the commotion?

QUESTION #38

"Are you so dull?" – Mark 7:18

Think about the butter knife for a moment (weird I know, but I promise that I have a point). If you were given the chance to be any knife out there, why would you choose to be the butter knife? The butter knife is no good for cutting, it is the least used of the flatware family, and even a fork can spread butter if necessary! The point is that the butter knife intentionally was made to be dull.

When Jesus asked the disciples around him why they were being so dull, he wasn't referring to them as stupid people. He was trying to help them understand that they were being ignorant about the things of God. We were not created to be dull; rather, we were made to be sharp with the very mind and heart of our Creator. In what ways are you being dull to the things of God? What is one dull area of your life that you can make sharp today?

QUESTION #39

"Why does this generation ask for a miraculous sign?" – Mark 8:12

I'm pretty sure that none of us has a Jesus Christ to-do list posted up on the bedroom wall. I wonder, though, how many of us keep a secret, running list in our hearts. Maybe that list begins like this: "I will really believe in Jesus if I see these things happen…." In Mark 8, Jesus actually refused to perform miracles for a group of people who only wanted to see miraculous things.

This question echoes an earlier question recorded by Matthew (see Question #22). These kinds of questions are recorded in multiple Gospels probably because each of the authors thought it was important. So again we are left with the question of being more concerned with the outcome of Jesus than Jesus himself. Could you be content today to just give your hopes and fears to Christ, knowing that he will influence the outcome?

QUESTION #40

"Why are you talking about having no bread?"
– Mark 8:17

Going to the refrigerator is a daily experience for most of us who live in America or in most Western nations. When we're younger, we never stop and think about how things got in there (mostly we realize when it's empty). In other words, we rarely think about who provided all that food. When Jesus asked this question about having no bread, he was helping to remind the disciples about the provider.

Back in Jesus' time there was a lot of talk about bread, and nothing would have been more memorable than feeding thousands with just five loaves of bread! The disciples (like all of us) would often lose focus on the actual provider because of being focused on the provision. As Jesus reminded his friends, the bread was not more important than the one who provided it. How do you need to have your vision refocused away from the provisions of your life (the things you want) and toward the provider?

QUESTION #41

"Do you have eyes but fail to see, and ears but fail to hear?" – Mark 8:18

Growing up I had a friend who was deaf. His name was Michael. Even though he didn't have the ability to hear, he definitely made up for it with his other four senses! In fact he was so good at his other four senses that I often forgot that he was deaf. My experience with Michael taught me that there are different ways to see and different ways to hear, which is what Jesus was getting at with this question in Mark 8.

If we're not focused on God—meaning reading his Word, communicating with God in prayer, and involving ourselves in discipleship—it will be very difficult to see what God sees or hear what God hears. When Jesus asked this question, he was not talking about a physical defect, but rather a spiritual one. Is there a chance that you are living with a limited form of vision and a limited form of hearing? Is it hard for you to focus on anything but yourself? How much more could you see and hear if it wasn't all about you?

QUESTION #42

"How many basketfuls of pieces [of bread] did you pick up?" – Mark 8:19

Have you ever worn braces—or do you have them right now? I'll never forget when I had mine put on. It was always hilarious to me when people would ask, "Did you get braces?" This question was so funny because it was plainly obvious to anyone that I had them; did they even need to ask? As I think about it now, I realize that my friends were just dealing with the reality of a change in my life.

When Christ asked about the basketfuls of bread that were left over from the miraculous feeding, he was helping to point out the obvious reality of what had just happened! The reality was that the disciples ended up with more bread than they started with—obviously Jesus had something to do with that. When looking for the miraculous in your life, start with something simple: How many basketfuls do you have? In other words, what is the obvious thing that God is doing in you today?

QUESTION #43

"Do you see anything?" – Mark 8:23

For those of us who don't wear glasses (yet, at least), this question may sound silly. But for those who do wear glasses, it makes all the sense in the world. People with poor vision know the difference between seeing and not seeing. The ability to see clearly is a universal concept. For example, no matter where you are, if someone loses their glasses, you feel compelled to help look for them. We feel bad for people when they cannot see. So does Jesus.

After Jesus healed the blind man in Mark 8, he asked a very important (and practical) question: "Do you see anything?" He asked this because he really wanted this man to see, so he followed up with his healing. Interestingly enough, the man couldn't see with great clarity so Jesus placed his hands on the man's eyes again to give him total clarity. Jesus is very concerned with people's physical well-being while on earth, so shouldn't we be as well? In what ways can you care for the practical needs of someone today?

"How long has he been like this?" – Mark 9:21

There are times in the Gospels when Jesus almost comes across like a psychiatrist or psychologist. His conversation with the father of a demon-possessed boy in Mark 9 is definitely one of these moments. The scene of this conversation between Jesus and the boy's father unfolded just as the possessed boy began rolling around on the ground and foaming at the mouth. Picture Jesus in the midst of it with his notepad and pencil, wearing square-rim glasses while sipping hot tea, asking a question like, "How long has he been like this?"

OK, that isn't quite how Jesus looked. But why would he ask such a question? Didn't he see the urgency of the situation? It's not that Jesus didn't care about the boy; on the contrary, he cared very much about him. That is why he took the time to ask about his medical history. Jesus would often take the time to get to know the people he was about to heal. Likewise, if we want to do great things in this world for Christ, we must not forget about the individuals around us. Is there someone in your life that you could take the time and get to know more about today?

" 'If you [I] can?' " – Mark 9:23

Do you remember that childhood story about *The Little Engine That Could*? He was able to pull his cars over a rather large hill because he kept telling himself over and over, "I think I can, I think I can, I think I can." It's a great story for kids but really has nothing to do with the way Jesus heals. As God in human form, Jesus had the ability to heal, and it was never anything that he had to muster up inside or the right combination of words that had to be said. Jesus could heal, plain and simple—but there is more to the story.

In Mark 9 Jesus was asked by a father if he could heal his son, to which Jesus replied, "If?" Seems like a rather arrogant question (as if Jesus asked it while raising one eyebrow in a condescending way)—until you consider the situation. Jesus' told the father that everything is possible for people who believe. This means that the real story wasn't that Jesus could heal, but whether or not the father believed he could. Jesus ended up healing this man's son, because the man said he believed. How might your belief (or lack thereof) in Jesus' ability play into healing?

QUESTION #46

"What were you arguing about on the road?"
– Mark 9:33

Small talk—everyone does it, right? Small talk is the talking that people do before they really start talking about something important (I suppose that should be called big talk). Nobody ever remembers the content of small talk nor should they, because in reality it's meaningless. When Jesus asked this question to his disciples, he was calling out the ridiculousness of their small talk. You see, they were just walking along arguing about which of them was really the best disciple. The disciples thought that this was important; Jesus recognized that it was merely small talk.

How often do we engage with Christ and never really get away from small talk? What do our prayers say about our ability to talk with God in a meaningful, mature way—or are even our prayers stuck in small talk mode? How can you move your interactions with your friends from small talk to things that matter? How would you answer the question, "What were you talking about at the lunch table earlier?"

QUESTION #47

"What did Moses command you?" – Mark 10:3

Take five minutes and list out the names of people who have positively influenced your Christian life the most. After you've listed them out take a minute and give thanks for each person; no doubt it is a list of pretty amazing people that God has allowed you to share life with. Have you ever wondered what Jesus' list would have looked like if he'd made one?. Would he ever be able to put anyone on that list?

Well, if Jesus' teaching is any indication as to who would be on that list, Moses would be near the top. Think about it for a second: As Jesus was talking to the disciples in this passage he was letting them in on who had influenced him. Clearly, Jesus knew the commands of Moses, and he expected his followers to know them as well. Jesus valued learning from others—especially those from the past. Of all the people that influenced you in the past, which ones might God be asking you to remember and value?

QUESTION #48

"What do you want me to do for you?"
– Mark 10:51

If you are even a little involved in your church (part of the worship team, attend youth group, usher on Sunday mornings), you understand the value of service and how people appreciate when you simply ask, "How can I help?" Imagine what your parents would say if you made it a regular habit of asking, "What can I do for you?" related to things around the house. In the same way Jesus seeks us out and asks, "What do you want me to do for you?"

This question must have been music to the ears of the blind man who heard it that day. Perhaps he had waited his whole life to hear someone say that. No matter how long, though, the simple question of Jesus was overflowing with love and compassion. Sometimes we can get so worked up with all of the things we can be (or should be) doing for Jesus that we ignore this simple question. Jesus asks you today, "What do you want me to do for you?" How will you respond?

QUESTION #49

"Do you see all these great buildings?"
– Mark 13:2

At some point in your life (if it hasn't happened already) someone will ask you the BIG question: "What do you want to do when you grow up?" Fifty years ago you might have responded by saying you wanted to be a firefighter, or teacher, or maybe even an astronaut. Today though, the job landscape looks different. Today young adults want to be a CEO, an entrepreneur, or a business owner. One of the main reasons for this shift is that money and security have come to outweigh purpose and meaning when dreaming about a potential career.

In Mark 13, Jesus asked a question that challenges our dreams and aspirations. The way the people around Jesus got caught up in the splendor of the big buildings in front of them could be similar to the way we get caught up in the overwhelming opportunities in front of us. The question to Jesus' followers back then holds the same weight today: In light of Christ's return how does a tall building (or a great opportunity) compare? How can you make sure that you always keep in full view the bigger picture and not just what the world puts in front of you?

QUESTION #50

"Simon, are you asleep?" – Mark 14:37

Have you ever fallen asleep in class, or at church? (Don't worry; it happens to all of us at one time or another!) Can you remember what caused you to fall asleep? Was it a late night, early morning, lack of a good breakfast? Regardless of how it happened, it probably had something to do with your schedule. Granted, math class may not be the most engaging thing in your life, but let's pick something else a bit more important or interesting—waiting in line for the concert of a lifetime, or experiencing the newest roller coaster at an amusement park. No one falls asleep while waiting for these things!

That's what makes this scene with Simon Peter in Mark 14 so interesting. Imagine being asked to watch over the Son of God during one of his most difficult moments on earth—and you fall asleep on the job! I'm sure Peter didn't want to fall asleep, but the reality is that our bodies have limits. You can only go so long without sleep, or survive for so long without proper food and water. A lesson Peter learned that day was that we must live our lives in such a way as to be awake and healthy and ready to do what Christ has asked us to do. What would happen if you lived your life in such a way that getting plenty of rest and eating healthfully was an act of worship? How would that change your daily routine?

QUESTION #51

"Why were you searching for me?" – Luke 2:49

I have lost each of my two children in a department store, and perhaps not surprisingly, they were both in the toy department when I found them! Yet this was not the first place that I looked for them. After I journeyed all through the store, only to be reconnected with them near the Lego® section, it should have been obvious from the start that they would've escaped there. At least, my two sons thought it would've been obvious! Similarly, Jesus (in one of the rare scenes of Jesus as a kid) thought it was weird that his parents searched for him for days only to find him in the exact place where the Son of God should be: in the temple.

Jesus wasn't surprised that his parents came looking for him; he was just surprised by how long it took them to find him. Jesus felt that his parents should've expected him to escape to the temple. Where do you escape? Where would people expect you to be: on the court, in your room playing video games, at the library? Would anyone be surprised to know you've been with Jesus?

QUESTION #52

"Why do you call me 'Lord, Lord,' and do not do what I say?" – Luke 6:46

Here is my absolute favorite church joke: "A teacher asked a kindergarten Sunday School class, 'What has four legs and a big furry tail, and lives in a tree?' To which one little boy raised his hand and responded, 'I think it's a squirrel… but I'm going to say it's Jesus.'" This is so humorous because as Christians we joke about Jesus being the answer to everything. We say it so much, in fact, that eventually, it almost sounds too corny to believe.

When Jesus asked this question in Luke 6, he was exposing a certain problem that some of his followers had: just saying Jesus was the answer without their lives demonstrating it. Much like the kindergartener who thinks Jesus is the right thing to say in any given situation, we can also spit out the necessary Christian lingo, which makes it sound like Jesus is our Lord. The real question is: Will your life genuinely reflect Jesus, or will "Jesus" be the punch line to a good joke?

"Where is your faith?" – Luke 8:25

Sometimes in church you hear people making statements like, "So-and-so lost their faith." Doesn't that seem like a silly statement—like if they lost it, then where did it go? Is it possible to "lose" your faith like you lose a retainer that you accidentally threw away in the lunchroom garbage can? Or is it more like when you lose your dog because the front door was left open? It is interesting that when Jesus asked this question about faith to his disciples, he was referring to faith as having been put somewhere else.

Here in Luke 8, the disciples were in a boat during a storm. Jesus was with them, yet Peter and the other disciples had their faith rocked by the strong winds and powerful waves. Faith cannot be lost (like something you can never get back), but it can be placed in other things. It's easy to do—even when the Son of God is right in the boat with you. How would today look different if you took your faith off of yourself—or off of your situation—and placed it on Jesus?

QUESTION #54

"What is your name?" – Luke 8:30

When was the last time you forgot someone's name? What was the situation like—were you introducing them to someone, or did they come up to you and say something like "Hey, remember me?" No matter the situation, I bet it was awkward. It's amazing how important a name is; just to hear your name called out, or used in casual conversation is so encouraging. In this Luke 8 passage Jesus took time to ask someone's name.

Jesus was remarkable in how he would take the time to get to get to know people. Whether you were rich or poor, healthy or sick (as was the case for Legion), knowing something more about the person he was interacting with was central to Jesus' ministry. Sometimes we think the command Jesus gave to love one another can be overwhelming when there is so much hurt in people's lives that we don't know where to start. If you're wondering how Jesus did it, sometimes he simply asked people what their name was.

QUESTION #55

"Who touched me?" – Luke 8:45

What was the last book you read? Did you like it? What was the purpose of the book? A great many books have been written about the meaning of Christianity, which is good because everyone asks himself or herself at some point in time, "What is the purpose of all this?" If we look at this question that Jesus asked, we might find an answer from an unsuspecting person.

Jesus was on his way to perform a healing at the house of a man named Jairus, but he was interrupted by a woman who touched him. At that moment Jesus stopped everything and exposed her act by asking who touched him. This woman had tried everything to get better, but after she met Jesus, she was never the same. What can we learn from a woman who has done everything she could—fighting all the obstacles around her in order to come in contact with Jesus? We can learn that our purpose is the same: to do everything we can to be with Jesus. How would your life be different if this was your purpose?

QUESTION #56

"What is written in the Law? How do you read it?" – Luke 10:26

On a scale of 0 to 5 (0 = never, 5 = all the time) what number would you say represents your Bible reading in an average week? Write that number down. Now, however much you read the Bible in an average week, using that same scale, what number would you say represents how often the Bible changes your life? Write that number down. Chances are your first number is higher than your second number. This is because most of us Christians are concerned by how much we read our Bibles, not how often it changes our lives.

From everything I've observed about Jesus, he would be more concerned with the second number (changed-life number) than the first. In this interaction with teachers of the Law, Jesus asked them *how* they read the Scriptures, not just *what* they read. How do you read the Bible: out of obligation or out of a desire for a changed life? How would your life be different if you were more concerned about that second number?

QUESTION #57

"Which of these three do you think was a neighbor to the man who fell into the hands of robbers?" – Luke 10:36

How many neighbors do you have? List their names out on a piece of paper. The average person would say that their neighbors are the people who live to the left and to the right of them (maybe they would include the family directly across the street, too). Back in Jesus' day there were no real housing areas, no cul-de-sacs, no apartment complexes— so when Jesus asked about a neighbor, to what was he referring?

Perhaps the term *neighbor* was referring more to an attitude of the heart than somebody's address on a mailbox. We tend to treat the people who live closest to us the best— mostly because we see them the most (these people are also the ones we usually call our neighbors). In his question following the parable of the good Samaritan, Jesus wanted to know which character treated this person with the greatest kindness, not who lived the closest to him! What if you lived your life this way? What if you treated other people the same way that you treat your literal next-door neighbors?

QUESTION #58

"Which of you fathers, if your son asks for a fish, will give him a snake instead?" – Luke 11:11

Do you remember when you were little and your parents would tell you to share a toy with your sibling or your friend? Even though they asked you to share, what you probably heard was "Release the toy—and give it to them!" This echoes one of our major misunderstandings in our relationship with God. This is why Jesus asked such an odd-sounding question.

Often we think that no matter what we want, God will not want us to have it. So when we hear people say that we should share things with God, we revert back to our childhood and hang our heads and say, "Oh, all right. Here, take it!" Jesus helps us to see that a loving father cares for his children and doesn't exist to give out rocks when children ask for bread. Knowing that God wants to share (meaning really share) in our wants, needs, and desires should be encouraging. How could this new way of relating to God change your prayer life? How would it change your interaction with the world?

QUESTION #59

"Did not the one who made the outside make the inside also?" – Luke 11:40

Probably the single, greatest innovation in candy-making history is the Blow Pop®. It is far superior to lesser lollipops, which only leave you with a soggy, wet stick once you've gotten to the middle. Not so with the Blow Pop, for when you finish the hard candy outside, you are left with a long, beautiful, gum-chewing experience. (The Tootsie Roll Pop® would be a close second, but even after a short while, the Tootsie Roll center is gone, too!) My point here is that the creator of the Blow Pop very intentionally designed both the outside and the inside.

Likewise, God didn't just create us to interact with our outsides so that we would only look like Christ-followers, but he intentionally designed our insides (our hearts, souls, and minds) to follow Christ also. The one who made you intended that your Christian life would be both an inside and outside expression. Do you address your inside just as much as your outside?

QUESTION #60

"Man, who appointed me a judge or an arbiter between you?" – Luke 12:14

Have you ever wondered why we don't respect mall cops as much as we respect the real police? I think it is mostly due to the fact that mall cops don't have the authority to do what real cops do—in other words, it's not in their jurisdiction. In this Luke 12 passage, where Jesus was speaking in front of thousands of people, his question implies that it's not in his jurisdiction to judge between people's financial dealings.

The meaning behind this question may not follow a general understanding that most Christians have about Jesus wanting to be involved in every aspect of our lives, but Jesus was saying that he wasn't appointed to serve in that role, so he wouldn't do it. Jesus came not to deal specifically with financial matters, but matters of justice, grace, and mercy, which should then be applied to earthly situations. How surprising is this question to you?

QUESTION #61

"How is it that you don't know how to interpret this present time?" – Luke 12:56

I read a story one time about a semi-truck that got wedged under an overpass. The stuck truck confounded highway workers as to how to solve the problem. As they were brainstorming complex strategies related to raising up the overpass to free the vehicle, a young boy rode up on his bike. The boy took a look at the scene and told one of the workers that they should just let air out of the tires until the truck was low enough to pass under! I have no idea if this story actually happened, but it is a great metaphor for common sense.

Sometimes we overanalyze things in our Christian life, and we can get very far away from common sense. When Jesus was speaking to a rather large crowd in Luke 12, he got after his followers for not being able to apply common sense to what was going on around them (he called it the "present time"). If God is the one who gave us our senses, it should not be uncommon to use them! In what areas of your life can you use some God-given common sense today?

"Why don't you judge for yourselves what is right?" – Luke 12:57

When was the last time you had to admit to something that no one else saw? Maybe you confessed to stepping out of bounds during a basketball game or leaving the overhead light on in the car overnight (which then caused the battery to die, thank you very much!). Regardless of the situation, responding in this way requires a ton of maturity.

When Jesus asked this question to the people gathered around him in Luke 12, he wasn't saying that their personal judgment was more important than his; rather he was telling them to grow in their knowledge of him. Jesus wants us to live in such as way that we know what is right or wrong because we already know what Jesus thinks is right or wrong. Just like we can judge for ourselves if we've stepped out of bounds, we can live just lives because we are Christ-followers. Where can you grow in your relationship with Christ so that you can judge for yourself?

QUESTION #63

"So if you have not been trustworthy in handling worldly wealth, who will trust you with true riches?" – Luke 16:11

At first glance this question from Jesus seems so obvious that it doesn't really need an explanation. It appears to imply that if you can't care for the little that you have now, you won't be given bigger things in the future—but something more may be at stake. In our lives we tend to believe that if we continue to behave the same exact way in the future as we do now, things will be automatically better. In other words, it's easy to be fooled into thinking that the issues or problems that we now have will go away with time.

Jesus used a question about wealth to help us see that we cannot expect greater things to happen in the future without dealing with things today. Whether it's money, self-worth, emotional issues, or something else, we must do the work with Christ now to see a change in the future. Besides, are the "true riches" that Jesus mentioned even actual things? What do you think could be better than worldly wealth?

"Where are the other nine? Was no one found to return and give praise to God except this foreigner?" – Luke 17:17-18

I remember seeing my math teacher in middle school shove an unreal number of pens, pencils, and highlighters into his top-right shirt pocket (which had a protector). Even though I was in sixth grade, I remember it looked rather silly taking up all of that space on his chest (Mr. Smith was a tiny, old man). Sometimes in life we collect up the experiences we've had with Christ like pens in a pocket protector.

When Jesus asked where the other nine lepers went here in Luke 17 and why they didn't come back to give thanks to their healer, he was exposing their ungratefulness. Nothing can be more ungrateful than to take a free gift from someone and walk away without expressing thanks. Likewise we have to be super careful not to collect up great weekend camp experiences or meaningful nights at youth group without giving thanks to God for those opportunities. The heart of Jesus' question is this: Are we just taking things from Jesus (forgiveness, mercy, physical provisions) without returning to him time and time again to say thanks for what he has done?

QUESTION #65

"Will not God bring about justice for his chosen ones, who cry out to him day and night?"
– Luke 18:7

What is your least favorite class in school? For many it is math or science, but for me growing up it was English. I loved to read and write; it's just that whenever I handed in a paper I would see "run-on sentence" written in red all over the page. It has taken me a long time to learn that in order to have proper grammar, you need things like periods, commas, and hyphens.

In this passage Jesus told a parable about a widow who was persistent in her prayers for justice. Jesus' question helps us to see that correct grammar is not always important when it comes to having a good prayer life. If we want to be able to pray without ceasing (as the Apostle Paul encouraged us to do in 1 Thessalonians 5:17), then we're going to have to do away with prayer always having a beginning ("Dear Jesus…") and an end ("… in Jesus' name, Amen"). In other words, how different would your prayer life be if it were filled with run-on sentences?

QUESTION #66

"When the Son of Man comes, will he find faith on the earth?" – Luke 18:8

Look around your bedroom. What things would you worry about *not* being there when you returned home at the end of the day? Probably the big things like a TV, a video game system, MP3 player, or even your pet turtle—but would you ever really worry about these kinds of things not being in your room when you got home? Usually we don't worry about it because they're always there.

If you want to know what Jesus worries about not being here when he returns, it's not things and it's not even people necessarily. Jesus is worried that faith will not be here when he returns. He worries that when he returns to earth, people will have placed their faith in the wrong things. Faith is a big deal to Jesus, and he talks a lot about it in the Gospels. How big of a deal is it to you today?

QUESTION #67

"For who is greater, the one who sits at the table or the one who serves?" – Luke 22:27

They say that if you're standing at the top of Mount Everest, when you look out you can actually see the curvature of the earth's surface. Now I know for a fact that the earth is round, but from a non-Everest perspective, it seems awfully flat. Your perspective at 29,029 feet is quite different, and in a sense you get a truer view of the earth because of it.

When Jesus was talking to his disciples in Luke 22, he was offering a new perspective on what it means to be great. Most people would look at the "one who sits at the table" as the greater of the two people, just like if you didn't know the earth was round, your perspective would tell you it's flat. Christ gave his perspective (the greatest perspective) on greatness when he paired it with the one who serves. What Jesus did by asking this question is like taking the disciples up to the top of Everest. Is your perspective on greatness similar to Jesus' view?

QUESTION #68

"Why are you sleeping?" – Luke 22:46

Have you ever returned home from something fun (or at least something that was supposed to be fun) only to realize that most of the excitement related to the event was in the anticipation of the event? Anticipation is often more engaging because as we anticipate an event, we will play out the best possible scenarios. For example, if I tell you we're going to the beach next week, you would never imagine it to be cold with overcast skies—you would imagine blue skies and a warm 85 degrees!

In this garden scene, as Jesus returned from praying, he may not have been as upset about the fact that the disciples fell asleep as much as he was frustrated with their lack of anticipation. Think about it: For the last three years of their lives, Jesus had been building them up for this moment— and where was their anticipation? In the same way, as Christians we're called to be caught up in anticipation for Christ's return. Are we awake? What would it mean to anticipate Jesus more?

"Did not the Christ have to suffer these things and then enter his glory?"– Luke 24:26

Take five minutes and list out all of the things that are necessary to sustain life. When you're finished you probably won't have a long list, but take anything off of that list (like oxygen, perhaps), and life cannot exist. It is hard for us to really identify with the suffering that Jesus had to go through, but what stands out more in this question is the idea of what was necessary. You can relate to *necessary*—just look at the list you made.

We may not be able to fully understand why Jesus had to suffer until we are with God for eternity, but we can faithfully believe that it was necessary. The reality is that if Jesus' death were not necessary for our salvation, he wouldn't have allowed it to happen. Likewise by Jesus asking this question, he challenged those who would rather take away the need for it (like Peter was prone to do). Do you have a hard time believing the sufferings of Jesus were necessary? Would others around you say that you believe that?

QUESTION #70

"Do you have anything here to eat?"
– Luke 24:41

List out all the things that truly happen "once in a lifetime." You might want to include things like a solar or lunar eclipse, the passing of a distant planet, or spotting Halley's comet. These kinds of occurrences are so rare that we often have unique preparations so that we can witness them (such as wearing a certain type of glasses for an eclipse or staying up late to see the comet go by).

In this Luke 24 passage, Jesus had just risen from the dead and was heading back to visit his disciples. Upon seeing Jesus' resurrected body, the disciples truly had a "once in a lifetime" experience—but the only problem was that nothing could have prepared them for seeing Jesus the way they did. We can't fully understand how the disciples must have felt in that moment, but we can be guaranteed there was a good bit of fear. That fear all went away when Jesus asked for something to eat. Thankfully, Jesus understands how to meet us where we are—fears and all.

QUESTION #71

"What do you want?" – John 1:38

Take a minute and list some of the great leaders throughout history. Why did you choose some people over others? (Maybe you included Abraham Lincoln on your list but not Thomas Jefferson.) Have you ever thought about what makes someone a leader? Some people try to attain leadership via an education or job experience or sheer talent, but at the end of the day, you are only a leader if someone is following you!

At the beginning of Jesus' ministry here in John 1, we read that Jesus turned around and saw two men following him. When Jesus asked them this question, it had more of a "Why are you following me?" feel to it. They were following Jesus because they wanted to learn more about the things he was teaching. Are you compelled to follow him because of a desire to be led by him? If so, you will likely hear the same question asked of you: "What do you want?"

QUESTION #72

"Dear woman, why do you involve me?"
– John 2:4

To be truly funny, you need a great sense of timing. All of the great comedians know that you have to be patient when delivering a joke so you build up the greatest level of anticipation, which will then get you the greatest response in laughter. Timing is also essential when playing sports; hitting a baseball, throwing a football, or spiking a volleyball all require proper timing. Jesus had perfect timing, and because of that, he saw amazing results.

In John 2 we have Jesus' famous miracle of turning water into wine. It all began as a request from Jesus' mother to help out with the wine-less situation. Jesus' initial response seemed cold and unfair, but he was more concerned about timing (namely his timing for revealing himself as Savior). Jesus' mother responded to this question by telling the servants to do whatever her son told them. In this moment she had a deep trust in her son because of his perfect timing. What do you need to trust Jesus' timing on for your life today?

QUESTION #73

"You are Israel's teacher, and do you not understand these things?" – John 3:10

Have you ever put a puzzle together? You know, the 5,000-piece puzzle that, once completed, makes a picture of the Eiffel Tower—or a basketful of kittens? The interesting thing about a puzzle is that everything you need to complete it is already inside the box, but it isn't really complete until you snap the last piece in its proper space. (BTW, it feels really good when you do that, doesn't it?)

Nicodemus was an intelligent person. He would've known the Old Testament very well; he knew the history and the prophecy concerning the coming Messiah. So when Jesus challenged him in John 3 regarding his lack of understanding, what he was really saying was that Nicodemus had all the right puzzle pieces, but he just hadn't taken the time to put them in their right places. What are you doing to make sure the same isn't true of you? How can you avoid only knowing the pieces of the puzzle, but never taking the time to put it all together?

QUESTION #74

"I have spoken to you about earthly things and you do not believe; how then will you believe if I speak about heavenly things?" – John 3:12

Have you ever fallen for this one: "Did you know that the word *gullible* is not in the dictionary?" Upon flipping through the closest dictionary, you immediately find that *gullible* is in fact there, and its definition reads, "Easily persuaded to believe something." Then you sheepishly realize that you have become the very definition of gullible—although being persuaded to believe in something is not all bad.

Some people, like Nicodemus in John 3, have a difficult time believing in things—even things other people know to be true! (Consider how you've probably used the expression "I can't believe it!" even after you've just seen something happen.) Jesus was telling Nicodemus that he must train himself to believe in easy things before jumping into things that are harder to believe. Are you a believing person? Are you easily persuaded to believe the things that Jesus says? Jesus would say to start with the small things first.

QUESTION #75

"Do you want to get well?" – John 5:6

I have heard it said that there is no such thing as a stupid question. I don't believe it because I have seen way too many people walk outside and ask if it was raining—while standing in the rain. Or the person who asks the teacher one minute before the bell rings if they were going to be assigning homework for tomorrow! Stupid question. Of all the questions Jesus asked in the Gospels, this one appears to be—dare I say this—stupid.

Jesus encountered a paralyzed man in John 5. He asked the man, who had been that way for 38 years, if he wanted to get well. It must have seemed like a stupid question to the lame man—of course he wanted to get well! But to Jesus it was not stupid; in fact, it was the perfect question (because everything Jesus said was perfect). Jesus never forces anything upon us; it is always a two-way street. What is not in question in John 5 is whether Jesus could heal; rather, it was whether the lame man wanted healing. Is there something that you are waiting for Jesus to do, without really wanting it in the first place? How does this question shape your desires?

QUESTION #76

"How can you believe if you accept praise from one another, yet make no effort to obtain the praise that comes from the only God?"
– John 5:44

Praise is a commodity. In other words, it can be given or received. For example when we "praise" other people (like popular sports figures and musicians), we are actually doing two things: accepting the right to praise, and giving them our praises. This sounds complicated, but it's as easy as watching ESPN or buying the latest chart-topping album on iTunes®. Giving or accepting praise isn't always a bad thing, unless we do it all the time—then it turns into worship. And Christians we ought to know how God feels about us worshipping other things besides him.

When Jesus asked this question in John 5, he was challenging the Pharisees to seek the praise of God. Think about all of the work we put into seeking the praise of one another, or how much money and time we spend giving praise to things we value here on earth. What if we were to give at least that much time and energy into seeking the praise of our heavenly Father? Praise is yours to give and receive—how are you using it?

"If you do not believe Moses' writings, how are you going to believe what I say?" – John 5:47

What is your opinion of science fiction? It's always been one of those genres that people either love or hate. For the people that love it, they *really* love it (meaning that they are willing to go so far as to stay out all night in line for the next great sci-fi movie or book release). But you have to give it to the sci-fi fans—they are totally committed to everything about sci-fi. If there is a book, they'll buy it. If there is a movie, they'll see it. If there is a costume, they'll wear it. They are committed.

Jesus was questioning the commitment of the Jews when he asked this question about Moses. He was telling them that if they were not even willing to believe the writings of one of their forefathers, how would they ever believe the things that he could teach them? (This would be similar to asking a true Lord of the Rings fan if they thought it would be OK to watch the films without first having read the books!) When we commit to following Christ, we also commit to what he has said. Jesus' words are to be believed and followed—even today. The real question is, do you know what he said?

QUESTION #78

"Where shall we buy bread for these people to eat?" – John 6:5

No matter what you do with your life, it is so important that you always allow for a bit of humor. Make a list of the five funniest people you can think of—maybe they're actors, friends, or comedians. What makes them funny to you? Is it their facial expressions, or their stage presence? I don't think that Jesus gets enough credit for being funny in the Gospels—especially since the Gospel of John tends to be more serious. This question that he asked to his disciples in John 6 is hilarious, though.

This passage tells of the miraculous feeding of the five thousand, which basically means that as thousands of people were converging on Jesus, he must have looked over to one of his disciples and asked where they were going to buy all the bread for them. The humorous part of this question was that there was no possible place where they could buy bread for so many people—even still, it must have been fun to watch Philip and Andrew squirm as they tried to come up with a legitimate response. What we learn in this question is that Jesus is real, with a real sense of humor—so how can this change your perspective of him?

QUESTION #79

"Does this offend you?" – John 6:61

When was the last time you were offended? Was it
something that someone said? Was it the way someone
acted around you? The reason something is offensive
is usually because it is displeasing or disagreeable. It's
interesting that when people are offended they will react
quickly—and with passion. Jesus knew that it wasn't wrong
to expose displeasure in the lives of the disciples, especially
if it caused them to respond.

As Jesus sat among his disciples in John 6, he knew that
some of them would struggle with believing in him (one
would even betray him). This did not distract him, though.
He continued to unfold his story about what would happen
to himself in his last days, and he knew that his story would
cause his disciples to respond with passion. Our lives do
not automatically line up with Jesus' teachings, because we
are imperfect humans. Have you ever been offended by
Jesus' teachings? How have the words of Jesus caused you to
respond with passion?

QUESTION #80

"You do not want to leave too, do you?"
– John 6:67

Have you ever felt abandoned? What was the situation? Was it something that you said that made everyone leave? Or was it something that you did? Regardless of the situation, being abandoned is no fun. For Jesus it was especially difficult because he was abandoned by the very people who had been following him. They were leaving him because his truth-filled teaching was becoming too difficult for them to handle.

As Jesus watched so many people walking away, he turned to his 12 closest followers (aka the disciples) and asked if they planned on leaving, too. What is so beautiful about this question is that it gives us a view into the honest despair Jesus sometimes felt during his time on earth. Jesus wanted people to follow him, because he knew what the consequences were if they chose otherwise. How does this question give you new insight into the life of Christ? How might it change your relationship with him?

QUESTION #81

"Have I not chosen you, the Twelve?" – John 6:70

Can you remember back to elementary school when you were out on the playground and had to be chosen for one of the kickball teams? Unless you were fortunate enough to be one of the people choosing teams, it was the worst feeling in the world to not get picked at the beginning. There is something so strong about being chosen for something, whether it's for the baseball team, the spring drama, or the group project for science class—there is power in being chosen.

In this emotional interchange with his disciples near the Sea of Galilee, Jesus asked an all-important question that reminded his best friends just how much he loved them. I like to imagine Jesus asking this question with hands outstretched, as he looked his disciples right in the eyes. In the same manner that Jesus chose the disciples to follow him, he has asked us to follow him. Therefore we must move from the thought that we *have* to follow Jesus, to the fact that we *get* to follow him! How will the fact that Jesus has chosen you to be one of his followers influence your life today?

QUESTION #82

"Why are you trying to kill me?" – John 7:19

Have you ever ruined a surprise? Maybe you spilled the secret about someone's surprise birthday party, or you accidentally talked about the gift that someone didn't know they were going to receive. Whatever it was that you ruined, it was probably because you forgot that the other person didn't know what you already knew. In John 7, Jesus asked a question that gives insight to something that a lot of people didn't know.

When Jesus asked the Jews why they were trying to kill him, they responded by asking him what he was talking about? Jesus was not trying to ruin the "surprise" of the crucifixion as much as he was trying to get the people to decide what they really believed about who he was. Not everyone responded to Jesus similarly in the Gospels; some people realized he was the Messiah, while others wanted to kill him, but the main question for us is: How will we respond to the reality of Christ's crucifixion? Will it make a difference in your life today?

QUESTION #83

"Woman, where are they? Has no one condemned you?" – John 8:10

Have you ever stood up for somebody? Do you remember the situation? Maybe you saw someone getting picked on and you felt like you needed to step in and defend him or her, or you befriended someone that no one else liked. While it may look like you were standing up for someone, you were really standing up for something. For example, you may not have known the kid on the playground that you stood up for, but you stepped in because you didn't believe it's right for anyone to be bullied.

Likewise as Jesus stood up for the woman in John 8, he questioned the Pharisees' understanding of who had the final say of what was right and wrong. In Jesus' mind, what she did was wrong (this is why he told her to stop sinning), but because he was the perfect Son of God, he alone retained the right to condemn her. Jesus did not condemn her because he was standing up for mercy. What are your definitions of justice and mercy? Do you know what Jesus has to say about these two things?

"Why is my language not clear to you?"
– John 8:43

Did you know that there are a ton of noises that the human ear cannot hear? One of the most famous examples is the dog whistle. The dog whistle is like any other whistle, except it emits a sound that only a dog can hear. The scientific explanation is that the whistle's pitch is so high that human ears cannot register it. The effect is that dogs run around in circles attempting to avoid the noise, while we keep blowing into a whistle that we can't even hear!

Jesus asked this question to the Jews in John 8—and then he answered it himself. It's pretty rare that Jesus answered his own questions (normally he asked a question, let the people ponder it, and then moved on to the next topic) so we must conclude that he wanted no confusion as to its answer. The answer is simple: They were unable to truly hear what he was saying. It's similar in principle to the dog whistle—because the people were trained to hear the noise of the world, they couldn't hear the things of God. Are the things around you keeping you from hearing the language of Jesus?

QUESTION #85

"Can any of you prove me guilty of sin?"
– John 8:46

There are lots of things on this earth that are difficult to prove. For instance there's the theory of plate tectonics or the theory of relativity or (my personal favorite) the theory as to why a pack of Mentos®, when mixed with a two-liter of Diet Coke®, creates an amazing explosion. Interestingly enough, though, when things become hard to prove they also become hard to ignore.

When Jesus asked this question in John 8, he was absolutely sure that no one could prove that he was a sinner. But he wasn't trying to prove he was perfect; he was just trying to get people to believe it. It is very difficult for us to prove that Jesus was sinless, but our inability to prove something focuses our attention and leads us to faithful conclusions. What roadblocks in your life might keep you from believing Jesus was without sin?

"If I am telling the truth, why don't you believe me?" – John 8:46

Can you remember times in your life when telling the truth was difficult? Maybe you confessed to throwing the ball through your neighbor's window or admitted your true feelings in a difficult situation. Telling the truth is not always easy, and for Jesus it often meant that people would ignore him and even disown him. The truth is not always an easy thing to tell, but it is powerful.

If Jesus' main goal on earth was to make a lot of friends, he wasn't going to get there by telling the truth. Even those who were closest to him struggled with his truth. Jesus asked this question because he was frustrated by people's inability to believe in God's truth. Jesus was willing to risk friends, popularity, and attention for the sake of truth. What is your value of truth? What are you willing to trade to ensure that the truth comes out?

QUESTION #87

"Are there not twelve hours of daylight?"
– John 11:9

I am a huge fan of the Christmas season. I like the way
everyone is more cheerful and gracious, I like the feeling of
goodwill in the air, and, of course, I love the yearly reminder
of Christ's birth. There is one thing I don't like, though: the
shortened amount of daylight. At that time of the year, it
seems like every day, you wake up and it's dark, and by time
you get home in the afternoon, it's dark out again! Doctors
say the lack of sunlight is one of the major causes of
depression in the winter months. There is something special
about daylight.

Jesus' question to his disciples in John 11 was both practical
and spiritual. Back in his day it was better to travel from
town to town during the day because you could see where
you were going—but we shouldn't ignore the parallel Jesus
makes here between physical and spiritual light. Physically,
life is just more difficult in the dark (you know this if you've
ever tried to make your way out of a room with no lights
on), and if we choose to live in spiritual darkness, we will no
doubt stumble along in our life with God. Are there ways
today that you can practically remove yourself
from darkness?

QUESTION #88

"Do you believe this?" – John 11:26

Have you ever jumped off a high rock into water or climbed a tree much higher than you thought you could've? These types of experiences are always memorable because at some point you had to push yourself to a place where you believed you could do them. Maybe a better way to say it is that you had you give yourself to it—because it's one thing to stand on top of that rock, but it's a whole different thing to jump.

When Jesus was talking here to the two sisters mourning the death of their brother, he asked one of them if she really believed that he could do what he said he was going to do. Sometimes we get confused as to the word *believe*—we believe in a lot of things, so what makes believing in Jesus any more important? Jesus' use of the word *believe* in this passage had more to do with giving yourself to something rather than just feeling it. What can you do today to give yourself to the things you believe about Jesus?

"Did I not tell you that if you believed, you would see the glory of God?" – John 11:40

If is a very small word that carries a large amount of potential. For example, if you do your chores, you can go out with your friends tonight. Or, if you go outside with wet hair, you will catch a cold. And my personal favorite: If you don't knock it off back there, I'm gonna pull this car over and…. Sentences that contain the word *if* seem to push us to action.

Jesus challenges our understanding of our relationship with God by using the word *if*. Most of us would say that seeing the things of God or hearing the voice of God is something that only older "super-Christians" get to experience. Jesus put it in a much easier manner. He said that if we believe, we could see the glory of God. What if we're too busy waiting to see God before we believe? Jesus would say we have it all backward.

QUESTION #90

"Now my heart is troubled, and what shall I say? Father, save me from this hour?" – John 12:27

Make a list of the five most honest people you know, and then ask yourself: Why do they stand out as being more honest than other people? After all, everyone is honest some of the time, but few people are honest all of the time. Actually, people who are very honest seem weird or out of place in this world, but shouldn't being honest be the normal thing?

In John 12 Jesus was close to the time of his crucifixion, and the question that he asked was an honest evaluation of his situation. In the next verse he concluded that there was too much at stake and he couldn't back out. I am so thankful that during his time of trial, Jesus didn't always smile and say everything was great. This should give us freedom to be honest with our lives. Is there something that you would like to be more honest with today?

QUESTION #91

"Do you understand what I have done for you?"
– John 13:12

Make a list of all the things that you understand. This shouldn't be a list of everything that you know—that is much different. For example, I know what basketball is, but I do not understand how to play it well. Maybe you know what a piano is, but you do not understand how to play Beethoven's Fifth Symphony. There is a big difference between *knowing* something and *understanding* it—to understand something means you have spent time with it.

When Jesus wanted his disciples to know what it was to be a servant, he didn't just tell them about it; he washed their feet. He wanted to make sure they understood it very well because this was what he was asking them to do. As we focus more on the life of Christ, we will move from a place of knowledge to a life of understanding. Where can you start doing this now?

QUESTION #92

"Don't you know me, Philip, even after I've been among you such a long time?" – John 14:9

Have you ever thought about how it might be easier for people to be Christians if Jesus was here in person, on earth today? Then we could talk to him and ask him any question we wanted—and his answers would no doubt win many people over! Interestingly enough, though, the disciples were with Jesus on a day-by-day basis, and still they struggled to comprehend what Jesus was saying.

Even though it would be so amazing for Jesus to be here today in person, the reality is that he has already said and done everything he needed to on this earth. Philip wanted just a little more evidence that Jesus was who he said, which is what made Jesus ask this question. But really this question is for us as well. Do we have enough to be able to say that we truly know Jesus after all this time?

QUESTION #93

"Don't you believe that I am in the Father, and that the Father is in me?" – John 14:10

What was the last fight you had with a sibling or your best friend? I can remember getting into arguments with my little brother, which would result in putting a line of tape down the middle of our room to divide up his side and mine. (The real reason older brothers do this, of course, is to keep younger brothers away from their stuff.)

In this question Jesus taught us that the line between where he ends and where God the Father begins is really hard to find. In other words, their relationship is so intimate that they are actually in each other (hard to explain, I know). Our relationship with Jesus gives us great access to the things of God because Jesus is not separate from him. How does this enhance your view of having Jesus in your life?

QUESTION #94

"Who is it you want?" – John 18:4

Make a list of the top 10 wants in your life (and be honest). Maybe it's a scholarship to a certain college, a car, or even a pet turtle. Why did you choose those 10 things over other options? There is a lot of power behind wanting something. Think about what lengths people will go to get what they want.

When Jesus approached the very men who showed up to arrest him in John 18, he asked a very simple but powerful question. Rather than ask what they wanted (which most of us ask when answering the door), he asked who they wanted. Even in his final days on earth Jesus was teaching others that the "who" is more powerful than the "what." (Remember back to the rich young ruler from Matthew 19 in Question #23?) What can you do now to make sure that you are desiring more of the "who" (Jesus) and less of the "what"?

QUESTION #95

"Shall I not drink the cup the Father has given me?" – John 18:11

My wife and I have now run two marathons together, and the one thing I've learned is that running the actual marathon isn't the hardest part. The hardest part is all of the hours spent (and the hundreds of miles run) preparing for the big day. It would be rather silly to do all of that, only to decide hours before the event that we really don't want to compete.

In a similar way, when Jesus responded to Peter's attempt to defend his Lord in John 18, he was asking him to consider all that had been done to get them to this point. Jesus had been training for his last days on earth, and it would be silly for him not to accomplish what he was preparing to do. That's why he got on Peter when he attacked with his sword. As we think about Christ today, we must remember that the cross was more than just a one-day deal; it was a fulfillment of much preparation on Jesus' part.

QUESTION #96

"But if I spoke the truth, why did you strike me?"
– John 18:23

List out some of the most recent decisions you've made and their consequences. Need some examples? *Decision: I studied an extra hour for my math test. Consequence: I got an A.* Or here's another one. *Decision: I forgot to show up for volleyball practice. Consequence: The coach benched me for the next game.*

Jesus made a decision in his life to tell the truth; the consequence: He was beaten. Something about this doesn't sound right, but honestly there was a lot about Jesus' life on earth that didn't sound right. Jesus did not come to earth to make logical connections between his decisions and his consequences. His only decision was to do what his Father asked him to do. How might this perspective of Jesus' life change how you view your own life?

"Is that your own idea, or did others talk to you about me?" – John 18:34

Have you ever thought about how much of what we know about Jesus comes from what other people tell us? If you grew up in the church, probably a large percentage of what you now know about Jesus comes as a result of listening to pastors on Sunday mornings, sitting through talks at youth group, or just one-on-one conversations with other Christians. While these experiences are all good ways to learn about Jesus, it is important that we take time to seek him out on our own as well.

In this John 18 passage, Pilate was asked whether or not his thoughts about Jesus were his own or if he had received them from someone else. There is no one who is disqualified from having his or her own thoughts about Jesus—not even the man who would ultimately help sentence Jesus to death on the cross. Jesus was constantly pushing people to engage with him and not just take everyone else's word on it. In what ways can you begin a more personal life with Jesus?

QUESTION #98

"Friends, haven't you any fish?" – John 21:5

Have you ever had an amazing weekend camp experience or a particularly powerful night at youth group, where afterward you expressed that you would never go back to your old lifestyle—but then you did? If so, you are not alone. It also happened to the disciples. When Jesus initially called the disciples to be "fishers of men," he literally called most of them away from being "fishers of fish." When they began following Jesus, they chose to abandon their old lifestyle. But they didn't all stick to it.

In John 21 after Jesus was buried and rose again, he went off to meet with his disciples. Some of those disciples, in Jesus' absence, were disheartened and confused, so a few of them decided to go out one night and fish. (Ironically, they caught nothing—just like the last night they were fishing before following Jesus!) When Jesus asked this question, he essentially challenged their previous decision to leave it all and follow Christ. It was a gentle reminder for us to stay the course and lean into our call to be Christ-followers.

QUESTION #99

"Do you love me?" – John 21:17

We end this book on a most important question—perhaps the most important question Jesus ever asked. We probably don't need to spend a lot of time talking about love except to say that love involves time, devotion, and emotion, and it usually results in a changed life. Jesus often talked about love—love for God, and love for one another. While it's not recorded a lot, I would bet that Jesus told his disciples often just how much he loved them.

Peter dropped the ball (big time) when he denied his Lord three times after his arrest. In John 21, they are reunited for one of the first times since Peter messed up. Jesus could have asked Peter any number of questions at that time. "Peter, what will you do to fix this?" or "Peter, you won't do this again, will you?" Thankfully, Peter wasn't asked a question like that, rather he was asked the question whose answer Jesus MOST cares about—and I close this book by letting Jesus ask it of you.

Jesus simply asks you this: "Do you love me?"